Joshua Haigh

The two martyred presidents of the United States

A book for bigger boys

Joshua Haigh

The two martyred presidents of the United States
A book for bigger boys

ISBN/EAN: 9783337142698

Printed in Europe, USA, Canada, Australia, Japan

Cover: Foto ©Suzi / pixelio.de

More available books at **www.hansebooks.com**

HONEST ABE

AND

BROTHER JIM:

THE TWO MARTYRED PRESIDENTS OF THE UNITED STATES.

𝔄 𝔅𝔬𝔬𝔨 𝔣𝔬𝔯 𝔅𝔦𝔤𝔤𝔢𝔯 𝔅𝔬𝔶𝔰.

BY THE

REV. JOSHUA HAIGH.

𝔏𝔬𝔫𝔡𝔬𝔫:

CHARLES H. KELLY, 2, CASTLE ST., CITY RD., E.C.;
AND 66, PATERNOSTER ROW, E.C.

1893.

MORRISON AND GIBB, PRINTERS, EDINBURGH.

CONTENTS.

———◆———

INTRODUCTION.

PAGE

The proper Study of Mankind.—Two are better than
one.—Nicknames, ...   9 12

CHAPTER I.

Birth and Early Training.

Home in the West End and the Far West.—Development.—Mothers the Main Instrument.—Means made
use of: the Bible.—Facilities for Knowledge.—Practical
Wisdom in the shape of Proverbs,   .   .   . 13-24

CHAPTER II.

The Lower Rounds.

Personal Endeavour. — Observation and Reflection. —
Manual Toil.—Done with their Might, .   .   . 25-32

5

CONTENTS.

CHAPTER III.

STILL CLIMBING.

PAGE

Moral Exercise.—Right *versus* Might.—Right *governing* Might.—Mental Culture.—Energy and Persistence.— Native Obscurity broken, ... 33-41

CHAPTER IV.

THE HIGHER ROUNDS.

Lawyer *et* Professor.—Thoroughly Honest.—Capturing Young Men. — Preaching. — Beckoned higher and made President, ... 42 57

CHAPTER V.

IN THAT FIERCE LIGHT.

Attaining and maintaining a Position. — Detestation of Jobbery.—The Man I have to live with.—Another Martyr, ... 58-61

CHAPTER VI.

WHICH FIERCER GROWS.

Southern Secession.—Lincoln's Conciliation.—The War inevitable through the Attack on Fort Sumter, . 62-65

CHAPTER VII.

BUT EVER SHOWS THE MAN.

PAGE.

Lines of Lincoln's Policy.—Position made difficult by his hatred of Slavery and the provocations of the Slave-party.—Further embarrassed by Slavery-sympathisers in England.—Still cheered on.—*Emancipation!*—The Rebellion crushed, ... 66-83

CONCLUSION.

The Cause of Humanity the Cause of God.—Stepping-stones of Difficulties.—Slavery under the British Flag. —To the Greed of others.—To Baseness in themselves. —Personal Freedom necessary to the Emancipation of others.- The Glorious End, ... 84-95

HONEST ABE AND BROTHER JIM.

———

INTRODUCTION.

'I am a man, and nothing that is human is foreign to me.'
—*Terence.*

THERE is an old but profoundly true line which says

'The proper study of mankind is *Man.*'

Other studies may be pursued—suns, serpents, rocks, rivers, moons, monkeys, satellites, stalactites : but they are uncongenial. Man is our fellow. His common nature and his kindred sphere make him one with us, and in his struggles and triumphs we may read and anticipate our own.

But why two men, and of all men, Americans, Yankees—men of brag and bunkum, who believe thoroughly in the aphorism :

> ' The man who in this world would rise
> Must either bust or advertise ' ?

Wouldn't one have been sufficient, and couldn't he have been found at home? No doubt. But the further the field the wider the view, and in matters requiring emphasis and confirmation two are always better than one.

At the entrance to one of our great rivers there are two lighthouses, one near the water's edge, the other on a rock behind. They are so placed, however, that when a vessel is right opposite the river's mouth, and may with safety attempt to enter, the two lights fall into one line, and the fact of their falling into one line is an indication to the captain that he may attempt to enter. And, similarly, if the lessons taught by the life of Abraham Lincoln are repeated in the life of James Abram Garfield, and if the lessons taught by the life of James Abram Garfield are anticipated in the life of Abraham Lincoln,—in other words, if the two lives in their great moral teaching coincide,—it is powerful confirmation of the truth of that teaching, and may inspire a measure of confidence in learning the same that we could not otherwise have.

One more preliminary thought. 'Honest Abe' and 'Brother Jim' are *sobriquets*, or nick-names, given to the individuals whom they respectively designate when boys, but which had so much of truth in them that they outlived the feeling that first gave rise to them, and clung to the men in later life. I have linked them together in the title of my book, not because I believe in nicknames, or am anxious to en-courage the feeling that often gives rise to them, but because in these cases they *hit off the characteristics of the men*. Abraham Lincoln had a large development of conscientiousness— a strict sense of truth and right and justice and honour—and may well therefore be called 'Honest.' James Abram Garfield had a large endowment of sympathy—a deep and tender feeling towards his fellows, especially those of them who were struggling and oppressed, and may well therefore be called 'Brother.'

It was these characteristics in them that made the men the uncompromising foes of slavery.   Abraham Lincoln opposed the foul thing, because he believed it to be unfair, unjust, and emphatically *dishonest*, for one man to hold property in another.   James Abram Garfield opposed it, because he recognised in every man a *brother*, and cherished a brother's feeling towards him.   And if we remember these things, despite the false or foolish feeling that often gives rise to nicknames, we may retain the present, and hail our heroes as

HONEST ABE AND BROTHER JIM.

CHAPTER I.

BIRTH AND EARLY TRAINING.

'Train up a child in the way he should go.'
—*Proverbs* xxii. 6.

'The mind follows the mother.'
—*Translation of Latin Maxim.*

AWAY in a wild, desolate kind of place in the old slave State of Kentucky, in the year of our Lord 1809, Honest Abe was born ; and twenty-two years later, in a similar place in the State of Ohio, Brother Jim first saw the light. Their surroundings were not sumptuous. On the contrary, they were bleak, bare, and unpromising—so much so, that if the boys at their advent could have taken them in, and have had the opportunity of saying yea or nay in reference to entering upon them, I can quite imagine they would have said *nay!* with a tone and an emphasis that would have daunted all gainsayers.

No house of stone, with plate-glass windows and mediæval or modern adornments, reared

BIRTHPLACE OF LINCOLN.

itself over their heads. No bed of down, hung with chintz and lace or draped with damask and *cretonne*, gave repose to their fair and delicate forms. No carpet from Axminster or Brussels yielded to the pressure of the servant's foot as she announced that the Rev. Augustus

Wigruff had called, or that Mrs. and the Misses Blazonby were waiting in the carriage to know how the mother and child were doing. No spoon of silver or mug plated with gold, the costly gifts of rich and devoted godmothers, opened their lips to daintily-prepared nourishment. No nursery of the fairy-land type, bedight and even made gorgeous with dolls' houses, Chinese lanterns, and illustrations of Jack the Giant Killer, Humpty-Dumpty, and half-a-dozen other different heroes, taught their young ideas how to shoot. The reverse of all that. Their home was a log hut, a rude enclosure of wood, twenty feet by eighteen, with a loft half-way across—very much like the hay-lofts of modern cow-houses—and which served as a separate bedroom. Their utensils were of the rudest—three-legged stools for chairs; long poles, with slabs, for bedsteads; sacks of hay, straw, husks, and dried leaves for mattresses; Dutch ovens for fire-places; and plates and knives and forks of wood : while their food and clothing were of the coarsest and scantiest.

This, however, is an age of development—a period of physical, social, and intellectual advancement : and when we are told, on considerable scientific authority, that the grandfather of the present noble Archbishop of Canterbury, some generations back, was a monkey up a tree : and that the great-grandfather of that 'Grand Old Man' who now holds the reins of English government, a little further back, was a grave old frog haranguing a parliament of frogs on the muddy banks of a pre-Adamic pond ; we are not surprised at anything in that line—not even when we read that Honest Abe and Brother Jim, who first saw the light in log huts, one of which was windowless, floorless, doorless, the other of which had large holes in the side covered with greased paper for windows—not even when we read that they ended their lives in the White House, the superb residence of the Chief Magistrate of the United States of America.

The main influence in this unwonted mental and moral development was that of the respective mothers. 'What France wants,' said the great Napoleon, when some one complained of the decadence of the national life, 'is *mothers ;* ' and most great and good men have been singu-

GARFIELD'S HOUSE.

larly favoured in this respect. That was the case with our heroes. Nancy Hanks, who became the wife of Thomas Lincoln, and Sally Johnson, who became his second wife, and Eliza Ballou, who became the wife of Abram Garfield, were women with heads on their shoulders, and—something in them. 'Mother, mother!' said a boy, bursting in upon the quiet of the house, rubbing his eyes and blubbering, 'all the lads say what a big head I've got.' 'Never mind, lad,' said the mother, intending to console him, 'tha's got *nowt in it.*' That was not the case with these women, though. They had not only heads on their shoulders, but something in them ; and that something they used in the training of their children. Their great aim in this regard was to *develop character from within them*—to make them intelligent, energetic, and good.

In pursuance of this object they read the BIBLE to them regularly. It was the constant practice of Eliza Garfield, whose husband died when Jim was only eighteen months old, to read four chapters each week-day of the week to her children ; and if no pioneer preacher came that way on the Sunday, she sought to

make the day bright and blessed by reciting
the stories of Cain and Abel, Joseph and his
brethren, David and Goliath, Daniel in the den
of lions, and the 'Holy Child Jesus;' whilst
Nancy Lincoln kindled the sentiment of liberty
in the soul of young Abe—a sentiment that
afterwards flamed up in the famous edict for
negro emancipation—by reading and re-reading,
expounding and emphasising, the story of Israel's
deliverance from the bondage of Egypt.

The women also gave their children all the
facilities which their limited means and out-of-
the-way situation could afford *for acquiring
knowledge.* These were not great. The whole
term of Lincoln's schooling did not cover twelve
months, though he is said to have drained four
teachers dry. And Garfield's term was not
much longer. But when you teach a boy the
three R's—reading, 'riting, 'rithmetic—you put
into his hand the key of all knowledge. There
is no limit to the possibility of his subsequent
attainments, save that which is imposed by his
own capacity.

Moreover, Widow Garfield sought to instil
into the minds of her children *practical wisdom,*

GARFIELD'S MOTHER.

in homœopathic doses, in the shape of proverbs
—wisdom which, she believed, would stand
them in good stead in the great crises of their
lives. One of her proverbs was, *Where there's
a will there's a way.* 'What does that mean,
mother?' said Jim. 'Why, it means this, my
boy, that if you make up your mind to do a
thing, although it may be difficult and well-nigh
impossible, you will generally succeed. Your
resolute mind will be both drill and powder
blasting the hardest rock.'

God helps the man that helps himself, was
another. 'What does that mean, mother?'
'Why, it means that when you have done the
best you can for yourself, God will help you as
He helped the Israelites when they had come
to the Red Sea, and could get no further.' 'But
does God ever help a man in anything but being
religious?' 'Certainly; He helps him in everything—running his farm, writing his book,
managing his business—everything that is not
sinful ; and He helps that man most who does
the best he can for himself.'

An ounce of pluck is worth a pound of luck,
was another. 'What does that mean?' 'Why,

it means that, instead of mooning about, in the hope that something will turn up, it's far better to go to work and *turn* something up. The stubborn glebe will yield thee weeds for naught, but it will only give thee bread in so far as thou dost compel it.'

In these ways did the mothers Lincoln and Garfield lay deep and broad and strong, in the mental and moral being of their boys, the foundations of a godly character.

CHAPTER II.

THE LOWER ROUNDS.

'Work for the good that is nighest.'
—*Rev. W. M. Punshon, LL.D.*

FAVOURING conditions and stimulating influences cannot supersede *personal endeavour.* We have machinery for most things :

> ' Propelling boats,
> Driving mills,
> Winnowing oats,
> Settling bills ; '

but I never yet heard of a machine for putting the multiplication table into a lad when he was asleep, or for drilling a boy, in the arms of Morpheus, in the Rule of Three, the Latin declensions, the dates of history, or the Tonic Solfa system. These things, if mastered at all,

25

must be mastered by personal endeavour, by the application and diligence of the pupil.

Such *application and diligence* Lincoln and Garfield gave. Soon as Lincoln had learned to read, he devoured his father's library, committing two-thirds of the volumes to memory. This was perhaps not so prodigious a feat after all, for the library only contained three volumes —the Bible, the Catechism, and Dibworth's Spelling Book. Garfield did much the same with his mother's library, which consisted of the Bible, the English Reader, and Davy Crockett's Almanack.

In the absence of a wider literary sphere, however, these boys did what every boy in America and England would do well to do, viz. *cultivated their powers of observation and reflection.* One day, soon after he had learned to read, Jim came across this sentence in a book, 'The rain came down upon the roof.' Immediately after reading it, he paused, looked grave, and then, with all the enthusiasm of a discoverer, exclaimed, 'Why, I've seen the rain do that myself, mother!'—an exclamation which shows that he had begun to observe and reflect.

He had observed, for he had seen the rain
come down upon the roof ; and he had reflected,
for he had turned it over in his mind to
such an extent, that when he saw a description
of it in a book he at once recognised it as
such.

Young men, would you be substances in the
world and not shadows, voices and not echoes,
perennial fountains and not extemporised
cisterns? *keep your eyes open, keep your ears open,
and brighten your brains by thinking.* Many
discoveries have been made ; but quite as many
remain to be made, and I don't see why you
shouldn't have a hand in making them. Ireland,
for instance, needs uniting to England—not
imperially but geographically, by means of a
tunnel under the sea. Then England will need
uniting to the Continent; and after that the
Continent to America. What an immense
advantage it would be if business men could
leave their homes in England on a Monday
morning, run over or rather *under* to America,
transact their business there, and get back to
their wives and families on Saturday evening!
What a saving of time and money! And why

not? There would be no *cow* on that line, the
great bugbear that frightened some of the
Members of Parliament when George Stephen-
son put before them his scheme for a line
between Manchester and Liverpool ; nor any
wayside station to stop at. Everything would
be plain sailing, so far as going under the sea
could be called sailing.

Then, again, mothers who cannot leave their
homes, and invalids who are confined to their
rooms, need the ministrations of religion—the
sermon, the lecture, the service of song. Why
not lay such ministrations on to their houses by
means of some telephonic arrangement, just as
you lay the gas and water on—to be turned on
and off at will? There's a sphere for your
energy, my friend, and your ambition too. Gird
up the loins of your mind, and address yourself
to it. And remember me when it goeth well
with thee ! When you have made your fortune,
and the world is ringing with your fame, just
give an extra sixpence to the ' Worn-out
Ministers' Fund,' in memory of a poor Methodist
preacher who had these ideas, but who was
precluded from using them by the law which

enacts that no Methodist preacher shall enter
into business!

Seriously, though, whether you are born to be
great discoverers or no, if you will only observe
and reflect—keep your eyes open upon what is
going on, and ask yourselves, 'What does it mean,
and how may it be utilised and improved?—
the process will give to your words and actions
an originality, freshness, and force which will
make you *men of power*, respectable and re-
spected, wherever you may move.

It is difficult to say at what period these
youths began *manual toil*. They seem to have
lent a hand and made themselves useful almost
from the time of toddling off. At any rate, on
or about the eighth anniversary of their birthday,
each was chopping wood, milking cows, shelling
corn, and 'choring' about generally. And they
continued their handicraft till they were twenty-
four or twenty-five. Not always in the same
line. Sometimes they were farmers, at other
times carpenters; sometimes black-salters, at
other times boatmen; sometimes store-keepers,
at other times surveyors; but in one form or
another working men—men who earned their

bread by the sweat of their brow—till they were some time past their majority.

Let no one sneer at that. In the present economy working men are necessary. Boots will get down at the heels and need mending; clothes will wear out and need renewing; houses will sink into decay and need repairing; and breakfast and dinner times will come and need providing for. Working men are *the sinews of the State!*

And what their hand found to do these working men did *with their might.* They did not labour under the vitiating thought, born too often of an overweening conceit, that manual toil was beneath them, and to engage in it a degradation to them. On the contrary, they believed that all toil, providing it to be honest, is honourable, and they had a manly pride in doing it.

This feeling led to *success*—immediate and, I believe, ultimate. When Jim was twelve years old, he was set to run his mother's farm. He had previously assisted his brother Thomas in this work; but Thomas went away, and the whole responsibility devolved upon him. This developed all the energy and manliness of his nature, and it wasn't long before the neighbours said to his mother, 'Your boy farmer is pretty lively, Mrs. Garfield; his farm looks as well as

GARFIELD WHEN A BOY.

that of any of us.' Soon after, he went to work for a carpenter at planing boards. During the first day he planed a hundred, and at the end of the day, as he stood with great beads of perspiration on his brow, had the satisfaction of hearing the carpenter say, 'They are well done.' Some time after, when he was attending the Chester Seminary, and working in the vacation to furnish himself with funds, he applied to a farmer for some mowing to do. 'Can you mow well?' said the farmer. 'You can tell by trying me,' said Jim. He did try him, and was so satisfied with him, that at the close of the day—understanding he was about to be a preacher—he said, 'If one of these days you *preach* as well as you mow, I shall certainly want to hear you.' And Abe did his rail-splitting, hog-killing, corn-shelling, and store-keeping with such thoroughness and satisfaction, that he commanded a man's wages when quite a boy, and earned the commendation of all for whom he toiled.

Young men, *don't despise the duty that lies nearest to you.* Get above the false pride, the radical littleness and vulgarness of mind, which would lead you to scorn the lower rounds of the ladder. To the majority of us, who are born at the bottom, they are the only means of rising.

CHAPTER III.

STILL CLIMBING.

'Patient continuance in well-doing.'
—Romans ii. 7.

THE manual toil of Lincoln and Garfield was educational in other respects than the development of their energy. It served to exercise, and by exercising strengthen, their *moral* faculties. When Garfield was fifteen years old he left home, and hired himself out as mule-driver on the tow-path of the Ohio and Pennsylvania Canal. This brought him into contact with a set of rough, brutal, whisky-drinking, whisky-loving men—men who had altogether more regard for the bottle than the Bible, and whose every prayer was an oath. So far was he from being corrupted by these men,

3

however, he was even enabled to correct, and in some degree elevate them.

'*Jakes, Jakes, what makes you swear so awfully?*' said he to a fellow who had been pouring out a volley of oaths one day; 'it certainly don't improve your conversation, and makes one think of Pandemonium.'

'Don't know,' said Jakes; 's'pose it helps to get some of yer bad stuff out.'

'Then, if that's the case,' said Jim, 'it ought to have been all out long since; for you have sworn enough to empty yourself times over. Instead of emptying, though, I rather think it helps to fill ye—the bad stuff in you growing by the cultivation you give it.'

'*What's the row*, captain?' said he to the commander of the canal boat, as they came up to one of the locks along with another boat, and when he saw the men springing to the tow-path in a most excited manner.

'Only a fight,' said the captain.

'A fight?' said Jim; 'but what about?'

'Why, as to who goes through the lock first.'

'But who came up to the lock first?'

'S'pose they did,' said the captain; 'but we shall get it, for our men are stronger than theirs.'

'But is that RIGHT?' said Jim, drawing his body up to its full height, and opposing himself like a wall of brass to the bare idea of brutal might triumphing.

The question stirred some latent elements of conscience in the captain. He at once and imperatively recalled his men; and the boat that had the right went through the lock first.

'*Give it him, give it him; pound him, pound him*,' said a number of men to Jim one day, when he had thrown a hot-headed Irishman, who had plunged at him like a bull for accidentally knocking off his hat.

'No,' said Jim; 'he is in my power, and I wouldn't lift a finger against him.'

Then, turning to the Irishman, he said, 'Had enough, Murphy? You can get up as soon as you say that you have.'

'Enough,' said Murphy.

Thereupon the two arose, when Jim went up to him, and, holding out his hand, said, 'I'm sorry I knocked off your hat, Murphy; it was a pure accident. I hope you'll shake hands and be friends.'

The two *did* shake hands, and were firm friends ever after.

Might governed by *right!* Power under the dominion of love !

Ah, Widow Garfield had *not toiled in vain!* Fourteen years before, as he lay a-dying in a log hut in the Western Reserve, her husband had said to her, ' Eliza, I have planted four tender saplings in these woods, and I must now leave you to *take care* of them.' And she had taken care of them—not only of their bodies, but of their souls ; not only of their minds, but of their morals. And here was the fruit. Her youngest son, a boy of sixteen years old, not only holds his own in truth and right and justice and honour against a set of brutal blackguards, but actually influences them for good. That was an achievement of which the angels might have been proud.

And Abe's conscientiousness and uprightness were equally tested and strengthened by the scenes and associations of his manual toil.

But while these youths were diligent in their

handicraft, and were deriving physical and even
moral benefit therefrom, they were *not neglecting
the cultivation of their minds.* Some girls *end*
their education at school; and it is said that
some boys are foolish enough to imitate them,

LINCOLN DEFENDING THE RED INDIAN.

for they speak of the last school they attend as
the one at which they 'finish.' That was not
the case with these boys, though. Not a tithe,
nor even a hundredth part of the information
they eventually became possessed of, did they
acquire at school. On the contrary, often after

a hard day of physical effort, and when many of their companions were sleeping, they were working—working to gain another round in the difficult ladder of knowledge.

'*Abe, Abe, put out that light and roll into bed,*' said Green Taylor, one of Lincoln's sleeping companions, ' I want to go to sleep.'

' Nonsense !' said Abe in his coolest manner; ' what's a sleep to the *History of the United States?*'

' Then if you don't blow it out, I will,' said the exasperated youth.

' You will ? ' said Abe tantalisingly. ' I'd like to see you. Perhaps you can manage it from where you lie ; you seem to have " blow " enough in you '—a sally that took all the wind out of Taylor's sails, and left Abe in undisturbed possession of the next half-hour.

' *What! studying grammar still,* Abe ? ' said another companion, who wanted him out for a run. ' What's your little game ? '

' To find out the kind of noun I am—common or uncommon.'

' Oh, I can soon tell you : you're an uncommon one, and an uncommonly uncommon one too.'

'Then, if that's the case, I must prove it by my uncommon diligence.'

' *Why won't you come out for a run,* Abe?' said another youth, who had been teasing him for half-an-hour.

'Because I mean to walk to Springfield and back to-morrow.'

'To Springfield and back! Why, that's forty-four miles.'

'Yes!'

'What are you going to Springfield and back for?'

'Look in at seven o'clock to-morrow night, and I'll tell you.'

The youth *did* look in at seven o'clock, and found that Abe had been to Springfield and back, had brought back with him four large volumes of Blackstone's *Commentaries on the Laws of England,* and had actually read forty-four pages of the first volume on his way back.

Ah, that's *the stuff of which men are made*—a firm-set will, a rock-built will, an invincible will—a will that opposes itself to all the temptations to ease and self-indulgence, as the ironbound coast opposes itself to the incursions of the sea!

Garfield was equally diligent with Lincoln in cultivating his mind. Soon as he had acquired the rudiments of knowledge, he determined to conserve and augment them by keeping *a school*. A committee man of Ledge, a neighbouring district, heard of this, and applied to him to keep theirs. At the same time he warned him that the scholars were 'a regular set of barbarians,' that they had already driven out two masters; and that, if he undertook it, he would probably have to stand over them with a cane, and thrash them all round. This was not a tempting prospect, and Garfield consulted his Uncle Boynton before accepting it.

'A tough piece of work, lad,' said his uncle; 'a tough piece of work! You see the boys know you, and have always known you, as *Jim* Garfield, and they will probably try to take advantage of you on that account. But if you can enter the school as *Jim* Garfield and leave it as *Mr.* Garfield, having quelled the turbulent spirits, it will be a regular triumph.' He *did* enter the school as 'Jim' Garfield, and he did leave it as ' Mr.' Garfield, having quelled the turbulent spirits; and he did it all, not by physical force, but moral suasion and the superior character of his mental endowments.

Thus—by buying up odds and ends and fragments and scraps of time, by often reading far into the night and even till the early morn, and by wearing the coarsest clothes that they might have money wherewith to purchase books —did these youths break the spell and entanglement of their native obscurity ; and on their thirtieth birthday, each found himself on the high road to fame—one being a leading *lawyer* in the city of Springfield, in the State of Ohio, the other being *professor of ancient languages and literature* in the Eclectic Institute of Hiram in the same famous State.

CHAPTER IV.

THE HIGHER ROUNDS.

'The path of duty is the way to glory:
He that walks it, only thirsting
For the right, and learns to deaden
Love of self, before his journey closes
He shall find the stubborn thistle bursting
Into glossy purples, which outredden
All voluptuous garden roses.

'The path of duty is the way to glory:
He that, ever following her commands,
On with toil of heart and knees and hands,
Thro' the long gorge to the far light has won
His path upward, and prevail'd,
Shall find the toppling crags of duty scaled
Are close upon the shining table-lands,
To which our God Himself is moon and sun.'
—*Tennyson.*

lawyer, a lawyer!' says one who shares
the conventional prejudice against the
class, and who believes that no good thing

PORTRAIT OF LINCOLN.

can come out of this professional Nazareth— 'that's disappointing. After all this talk about mental and moral development, we expected something superb—a minister at least, perhaps something better ; and now to turn off with a lawyer—one who cudgels his brains to cheat his fellows, and who, if he swallow half-a-sovereign, can never, even under the pressure of the stomach-pump, be made to disgorge more than three-and-fourpence of it—disappointing !' But there can be *good* lawyers as well as good ministers ; and the fact that perhaps they are not over-plentiful is a reason—and a powerful reason too —why Honest Abe and men of kindred spirits should join their ranks. At any rate, Honest Abe *did* join their ranks, and, I believe, retained his honesty therein.

'Mr. Lincoln, I want you to undertake my case,' said a gentleman, stepping into his office and accosting him one day. 'Be pleased to state it,' said Lincoln. So the man began. He hadn't proceeded far, however, before Lincoln interrupted him, saying, 'Excuse me, sir, I'm sorry to interrupt you ; but I'm bound to tell you I cannot undertake your case. I already perceive from your own statement of it that you are in the wrong.'

'But that's no business of yours,' said the man, 'providing you get jolly well paid for it.'

'Indeed, but it is my business. I never knowingly undertake to defend a wrong case.'

'But at any rate you can make bother for the other party.'

'No doubt I could ; in fact, I have no doubt if I undertook your case I could win it for you —*i.e.* I could extort five hundred dollars from a poor widow who has a large family dependent on her, and put it into your pocket. But I *won't do it*—not for any money! And here I tender you a piece of advice gratuitously. You seem to be a smart, capable, clever kind of man : go to work and *earn* five hundred dollars honestly, instead of trying to extort it from somebody else.'

That was noble, and it was the uniform principle on which Lincoln transacted his legal business.

Garfield, in his professor's chair at Hiram, was a *man of power*. He had long cultivated those elements of character which were calculated to give him a commanding influence over his fellows, and here he had every opportunity of exercising them. One of his strong points—a point on which he prided himself—was his penetration, his deep insight into human nature—a penetration, an insight, which he used with marvellous effect.

It *is* said that there are different ways of managing the ordinary donkey, the four-legged one, but that one of them is better than another. You may *belabour* or *beguile* it. You may stand over it with a stout stick, and beat it most unmercifully; in which case, in all probability, the animal will simply straddle its legs, throw back its ears, and stand stock-still. Or you may mount its back, and at the end of a long pole dangle a few inches before its nose a rich, ripe, toothsome-looking, savoury-smelling carrot; in which case, in all probability, it will bear you whithersoever you will.

And just so is it with the extraordinary donkey, the two-legged one. You may *lure* and *lead* where you cannot *drive*. Garfield knew this, and was often on the luring tack. Take one instance.

Scene. —The President's Study at the Hiram Institute.
Time. —Late in the afternoon of a hot day in June.
Dramatis Personæ. — The President himself, and a Mr.
Crawford—a big, burly-looking Western Reserve farmer.

Garfield.   Good   evening,   Mr.   Crawford.
I'm glad to see you.   I wanted to have a little
talk with you about Henry.   I hope you intend
him to return for the autumn term?

*Farmer (very deliberately and with a strong
nasal accent).*   Wal, ez to thet, Mr. Garfield, I
reckon not.   I giss I can't afford to sin' him
any more.   He's got eddicashon enuf fer a
farmer already, and I notice thet wen they gits
too much, they sorter gits lazy loike.   Yer
eddicated farmer's no good, Mr. Garfield.   He's
a reg'lar humbug.

Garfield.   Indeed ; I'm sorry to hear you
say that, Mr. Crawford.   I know that Henry
has been considerable expense to you, but I had
hoped he might come back for the autumn term,
and thus be in a position to do something towards repaying you.

Farmer (with a puzzled look).   Indeed —
repayin' me !   Wat du you mean, Mr. Garfield?

Garfield.   Well, you see, by the time the
autumn term is through, the winter will be upon

PORTRAIT OF GARFIELD.

us. Now, Henry could not work on the farm
in the winter; but if he came back for the
autumn term, he might take a school and earn
some money for you.

*Farmer (looking very much as though a new
light had dawned upon him).* Ah! thet's a
horse of anither colour, Mr. Garfield. Wal, the
lad wants to come bad enuf; I giss I'll hev to
lit him.

[*Exit farmer*—persuading himself that he has done a
generous thing in consenting to Henry's return; but
having really been beguiled by Garfield, who, understanding his covetous nature, had dangled dexterously
before his eyes the *rich, ripe, golden carrot.*

And in this way Garfield captured many a
young man—captured him from the grinding
avarice of his father, from the uncongenial
calling to which that avarice would have doomed
him, and from the life of obscurity, and perhaps
positive misery, that would have been the result.

At Hiram, too, Garfield devoted himself to
the work of *preaching.* Ten years before, when
mule-driver on the tow-path of the Ohio and
Pennsylvania Canal, he had a narrow escape from
being drowned. He fell into the water one
night. It was pitchy dark. No one saw him;

no one heard him. When he had come up for the second, and was about to go down for the third, and—as we commonly say—the last time, he threw out one of his hands, which by accident, as it seemed, came into contact with a rope. One of the ends of the rope was lying on the deck of the vessel. It was lying loose, however, so that, when Garfield began pulling at it, it began to come away. Just before it had come away entirely, however, and by the merest accident again, as it seemed, a kink in the rope caught in a crack in the side of the boat, and held, and hand over hand he drew himself out. It seemed almost miraculous, and Garfield was powerfully impressed by it.

Shortly afterwards, he had a severe attack of ague, which drove him to his home. While there, under the kindly, gentle influence of his Christian mother, he *gave his heart to God*, and became a decided and earnest CHRISTIAN ; and ever after it was his delight, as he had opportunity, to

> ' Tell to those around
> What a dear Saviour he had found ;
> To point to Christ's atoning blood,
> And cry, " Behold the way to God ! " '

Garfield was perfectly contented with his position at Hiram. He wrote to a friend soon after attaining it : ' I have now reached the height of my ambition, and here would I live and die.' God ordained it otherwise, however. Just then the slavery question was to the fore in the States, and the whole Union was agitated by it. Advocates for and against the foul thing were stumping the land and stirring up the minds of the people. Garfield was against it—against it both by training and conviction. As a boy he had read in his mother's Bible, in a log hut in the Western Reserve, ' And hath made of one blood all nations of men for to dwell on all the face of the earth.' As a youth he had read in the religious poets :

> ' Fleecy locks and black complexion
> Cannot forfeit nature's claim ;
> Skins may differ, but affection
> Dwells in white and black the same.'

And he believed these things—believed them with a depth and intensity of conviction that would not suffer him to rest when he heard the rights of the negro questioned.

His utterances in defence of the negro brought

him into the political arena. The Anti-Slavery
party saw that in him they had a man of power,
a 'great gift of God;' and they determined to
use him. They therefore elected him to the
State Senate in 1860, to the United States
Congress in 1862; and, eighteen years after—
having served his country in peace and war, by
pen and sword—he found himself at the *top* of
the social ladder, and was proclaimed

PRESIDENT OF THE GREAT REPUBLIC!

Lincoln's case was somewhat different. He
was, both by choice and circumstance, much
more of a politician than Garfield. As a boy
he had read the lives of Washington and Henry
Clay—Washington, the founder and first president of the great Republic, and Henry Clay,
one of its brightest ornaments. As a youth
he had both 'spouted' and written politics—
spouted them among his companions, and written
them in a local organ. And he even suffered
himself to be nominated for the State Senate
before he had fixed his profession, and when
there was little likelihood of his being elected.
Not that he was self-seeking or meanly

THE WHITE HOUSE, WASHINGTON.

[*Photo by* C. W. Bell.

ambitious. He was not. But he had a natural
love for politics—a love almost amounting to a
passion; and such ability as God had given
him he determined to consecrate to his country
along political lines. He was therefore elected
to the State Senate in 1834, to the United
States Congress in 1846; and, sixteen years
after — having established a reputation for
thoroughness, integrity, good judgment, and
sound sense, such as has seldom been equalled—
a reputation which even the stress and strain of
a great rebellion could not impair — he was
beckoned higher; and the

FORTUNES OF FORTY MILLIONS OF PEOPLE,

WITH THE

DESTINY OF A GREAT AND GROWING REPUBLIC,

WERE PLACED IN HIS HANDS.

The chrysalides have cracked into shining
wings! The inner impulse of native worth has
burst the bar of circumstance! And Honest
Abe and Brother Jim, than whom few have
started life more humbly or obscurely, have

> ' Mounted up from high to higher,
> Till now, on *Fortune's crowning slope*,
> They stand, a lofty people's hope,
> *The centre of a world's desire!*'

CHAPTER V.

IN THAT FIERCE LIGHT.

' O polished perturbation ! golden care !
That keep'st the ports of slumber open wide,
To many a watchful night ! '
                                        —*Shakespeare.*

' What is a king? A man condemned to bear
The public burthen of a nation's care.'
                                        —*Prior.*

IT's one thing to go up, another to keep up ;
one thing to attain a position, another to
maintain it. The rocket goes up—grandly,
gloriously, and with a flourish and demonstra-
tion that almost seem to extinguish the stars.
But it comes down again—with a blackness and
degradation that are in perfect contrast. And
just so is it with some men. They are thrown
to the front by a combination of circumstances,
and all eyes are fixed upon them. But it is

only to see them disappear — shamefully, ignominiously.

That was not the case with these men, though. They were as great in prominence as in obscurity, in the sunshine as in the shade, on the lofty and responsible heights of power as in the quiet and secluded valleys beneath. They had so many and such sterling qualities—qualities of brain and of body, of mind and of heart — that they could scarcely be *mis*placed, and prominence and position only gave them scope and occasion.

The term of Garfield's presidency was brief, only four months; but quite long enough to attest his competency. One of the great curses of American political life, a curse which had clung to it for years, and deeply degraded it, was its *jobbery*—its subordination of great public ends to objects of personal ambition. Men who were not conspicuous for their ability, but who were bold and unscrupulous, could often work their way into positions of prominence by rendering themselves useful and almost necessary to others. Garfield saw this, and determined to aim a blow at it. His own election had been independent of such influences, and on the night of his return for the State Senate he could fearlessly declare, ' It has been the plan of my life to follow my convictions of right, at whatever personal cost. While not unmindful of the approbation of others, I have been anxious, above all things else, to secure the approbation of *myself.* I have to *live* with myself—eat, drink, lie down and sleep, and I shall eventually have to *die* with myself: if, therefore, I would have peace of mind, I must have the approval of my own conscience.'

And was this the time to abandon the lofty plan, when it might be most influential for good? Nay, nay! That would have been to undo the work of a lifetime in one short hour. Garfield knew this. In selecting his Cabinet, therefore, he subordinated personal and party to great public ends, and called those men—and those men only—who, he believed, would serve the public good.

This gave great dissatisfaction, especially to the place-hunters; and one of these, Charles James Guiteau—a lawyer of French extraction practising in Chicago—was so moved by his dissatisfaction as to vent it through the chambers of the revolver. He *shot* the brave man; and God had another MARTYR!—a martyr to conscience as opposed to convenience, to principle as opposed to mere policy!

TOMB OF GARFIELD.

CHAPTER VI.

WHICH FIERCER GROWS.

> ' A monarch's crown,
> Golden in show, is but a crown of thorns,
> Brings dangers, troubles, cares, and sleepless nights.'
> —*Milton.*

> ' Oh, unhappy state of kings !
> 'Tis well the robe of majesty is gay,
> Or who would put it on ? A crown ! what is it ?
> It is to bear the miseries of a people !
> To hear their murmurs, feel their discontents,
> And sink beneath a load of splendid care !
> To have your best success ascribed to fortune,
> And fortune's failures all ascribed to you !'
> —*Hannah More.*

THE term of Lincoln's presidency was longer than that of Garfield, and so important that it may be said to mark an *era*—and a very important one too—not only in the history of the United States, but in the history of a subject race.

For, long before his election, the South— slave-owning and slavery-loving—had had a preponderating—not to say controlling—influence in the Legislature, and the Supreme Court had done little but register Southern decrees. Now, however, it seemed as though that influence were about to be checked. Not that Lincoln had given pledge, or even sign, that he would check it. On the contrary, he had declared before his election that, if elected, he should feel bound to recognise slavery where it existed, to uphold the Fugitive Slave Law where it was in force, and to abstain from officially interfering with that, as with any other acknowledged and important State institution.

But these traffickers in flesh and blood were not satisfied with this. They had been accustomed to have their own way so long and to such an extent, that the bare idea of having a man at the head of affairs who did not sympathise with their 'darling institution,' enraged them ; and before his inauguration in spring they *seceded*—angrily withdrew from the Union, founding another Republic on the basis of slavery.

Lincoln did all he could to conciliate them. He thought that secession might be the effect of a momentary irritation, which time and a little patient kindliness on his part would allay. He therefore announced that if South Carolina, which had headed the secession, did not obstruct the collection of port revenues, or break any other Federal law, she would not be out of the Union, and there would be no trouble. But South Carolina *did* obstruct the collection of port revenues ; and more than that—on April 12th, 1861, that memorable April 12th—she *opened fire on Fort Sumter*, one of the Federal forts, where the commandant had concentrated his troops. That was the *gage of battle*. Preventible before, the bloody thing was inevitable now. And so it came to pass that 'with hatred in their breasts, and the weapons of murder in their hands, the two brothers stood face to face.'

Into the details of that terrible four-years' fratricidal strife—a strife the like of which few nations have known, and none may ever wish to know—I shall not enter here. They may be read in a dozen histories. What I want is to fix your attention on *Lincoln* — Lincoln who of all men had weight and responsibility therein.

CHAPTER VII.

BUT EVER SHOWS THE MAN.

'. . . . . We come to know
Best what men are in their worst jeopardies.'

—Daniel.

'If thou canst plan a noble deed,
  And never flag till it succeed,
  Though in the strife thy heart should bleed :
  Whatever obstacles control,
  Thine hour will come—go on, true soul !
  Thou'lt win the prize, thou'lt reach the goal.'

—Mackay.

'Out from the land of bondage 'tis decreed our slaves
    shall go,
And signs to us are offered, as before to old Pharaoh ;
If we are blind, their exodus, like Israel's of yore,
Through a Red Sea is doomed to be, *whose surges are
    of gore.*'

—Lowell.

LINCOLN entered upon that terrible strife
with three great convictions :—

(1) That it was his duty, as President, to
maintain the Union ;

(2) That, if possible, he ought to maintain
the Union *without interfering with State rights ;*
but

(3) That its maintenance was so important,
that, if necessary, *State rights must be made to
give way before it.*

And are not these convictions right? I am
not a lawyer, nor even a politician; but I trust
I am not absolutely blind in matters of moral
colouring, and it certainly seems to me that
they are.

Take the first—the duty of the President to
maintain the Union. Who can doubt that?
He was not the President of South Carolina,
or Mississippi, or Louisiana, or any separate
seceding State. He was the President of the
UNION—the thirty-four States that had con-
sented together, and collectively formed the
great Republic ; and for him to have stood by
and seen the Union disintegrated, by State after
State withdrawing therefrom, would have been
an act of *treason in high places*—base, perfidious,
damning in the extreme !

Take the second—the duty of the President,
if possible, to maintain the Union without

interfering with State rights.   That cannot be
doubted, as against Lincoln.   It was, if anything,

LINCOLN IN A COUNCIL OF WAR.

favourable to the slave-party.   At any rate, it
was in the direction of *conciliation.*

Take the third—the duty of the President to maintain the Union, even if he had to interfere with State rights in so doing. That, it seems to me, cannot be doubted either. If the whole be greater than a part, if the Union be above the State, and if, as our Saviour teaches, the body is more than one of its members, then it is right, it must be right, to *puncture an offending member* —to interfere with its rights, even though it be its right to hold slaves, rather than that the whole body politic should be cast into the hell of disintegration.

These were the convictions along the lines of which Lincoln projected his policy, and to which, throughout the whole of that four-years' terrible struggle, he faithfully adhered. He announced at the outset that his object was to *save the Union.* 'If there be those,' said he, 'who would not save the Union unless they can save slavery, I do not agree with them. If there be those who would not save the Union unless they can destroy slavery, I do not agree with them. I am

PRESIDENT OF THE UNITED STATES,

and I conceive it to be my first duty *not* to be *faithless* to my trust.'

For three years he struggled to save the Union, *without interfering with State rights.* This, we may well believe, was a hard task.   He hated slavery with a perfect hatred—so perfect, that if his body had been gunpowder, he would willingly have bequeathed it to blow up the foul thing.

Had he not read of the *horrors* of ' the middle passage,' as it was called—the passage from Africa to America ; where human beings, with souls in their bodies, were crowded together like so much cargo—crowded in a sitting posture, with their knees pressed close against their breasts—and crowded so closely that they could not stir, could scarcely breathe, and where many of them died of sheer suffocation ?

Had he not read, too, of the *outrages* of slave-owners—how they frequently lopped off the ears, cut off the fingers, chopped off the toes, and burnt the initials of their names into the cheeks of their human property ; and how they acknowledged these outrages in the public prints, as a means of identification, when that human property had run away ?

Had he not read, further, of the *degradation of*

THE SLAVE AUCTION.

feeling among the slave-owners—how they would
frequently beget children of their female property
that they might sell them into slavery; and how
they would continue to do this, when the poor
pretext of human passion had died down within
them, and there was no other motive for it than
the ' despicable love of gain?'

And had he not read once again of the *shield
and encouragement* which the *law gave* to these
ruffians, whilst it afforded next to no protection
to the slave? Did he not know that, in many
of the States, the law expressly protected the
master in the use of the cow-hide and the whip;
that in the State of South Carolina it pro-
vided that any one might kill an escaped slave
who refused to surrender, without any accusation
or impeachment of crime; and that in every
State it warranted a justice of the peace in
arresting a coloured man whom he met in the
streets, laying him in irons, putting him in prison
and advertising him; and although the man
might have earned his freedom by some signal
act of devotion, if no one claimed him, in a given
time it warranted the dignitary in selling him
to defray the expenses of his arrest?

And did he not know that the law which
dealt thus liberally with the master, *denied
entirely the rights of the slave*, especially his
right to *hold property?* Had he not read of the
famous Mississippi case, in which a planter, out
of pure gratitude, married a negress who had
nursed him through a long and virulent disease,
had a large family by her, and upon his death
bequeathed his estates to her and her children ;
but in which the law came in and said, ' This
will is a *fraud upon slavery*—coloured people
cannot hold property ; on the contrary, they
themselves are property ;' and in which it
decreed that the estates must pass to the
deceased man's brother, while the wife and
children must pass into slavery ?

Lincoln knew all these things—knew them
too well ; and the measure of his knowledge of
these things was the measure of his difficulty in
holding hands off slavery.

Moreover, the *conduct* of the slave-party was
aggravating in the extreme. A leading Southern
newspaper spoke of ' that abominable and hellish
doctrine of Abolition, repugnant alike to God
and reason ;' while a writer in the same paper

demanded, ' Shall Abe Lincoln, the Abolitionist,
be permitted to set foot on Southern soil?'
replying, ' Never! I, as one of thirty thousand,
will volunteer to butcher the villain.' A member
of the House of Representatives from South
Carolina warned all Abolitionists that, if ever
chance should throw them into their way, they
would receive a felon's death. Vigilance com-
mittees were established all over the South, and
rewards were publicly offered for the heads of
known or suspected Abolitionists; while the
government of South Carolina recommended
the summary execution, without even the
benefit of a clergyman, of all holding anti-
slavery views.

And these were *not empty threats.* Tarring,
feathering, arresting, imprisoning, flogging,
maiming, and even worse outrages, were common.
The Rev. James Lovejoy, an Abolitionist of
Alton, Illinois, was shot dead in his office; seven
Abolitionists were hanged in one day at Talla-
hatchie, Mississippi; and it was declared that
if Dr. Channing—the great champion of the
rights of man *as man*—were to enter South
Carolina, even though he did it with a body-

guard of twenty thousand, he would never come out alive.

Still, notwithstanding his hatred of slavery, and the provocations of the slave-party, Lincoln was so anxious not to give the latter the slightest pretext for secession, that for three years he struggled to restrain himself in regard to the former.

Towards the end of that time, however, it became fully apparent that he ought to restrain himself no longer. Blow after blow, stroke after stroke, had descended on the guilty land ; and each one, as it fell, seemed, like one of the plagues of Egypt, to say, 'Let my people go.' Big Bethel said, 'Let my people go.' Bull Run said, 'Let my people go.' Gettysburg said, 'Let my people go.' And all, taken together, made a chorus of demand louder, and more imperative, than the multiplied plagues of Egypt, 'Let my people go !'

The South, in its heads and representatives—Jefferson Davis and Alexander H. Stephens—said, 'You daren't let them go ; you shan't let them go. The negro is not the equal of the white man. Slavery, subjugation to the superior

LINCOLN AND HIS SON READING THE BIBLE.

race, is his natural and normal condition. And on this obvious physical and moral truth we take our stand, and *defy* you to let them go.'

'The Toryism, official Whiggism, and half-hearted Liberalism of England,' represented by that powerful but occasionally crusty curmudgeon, Thomas Carlyle, said, 'You oughtn't to let them go; you mustn't let them go; it would be *unrighteous* to let them go;' and straightway unfolded its parable thus :

PETER and PAUL met together one day—PETER representing the North, PAUL representing the South.

Peter. Paul, you unaccountable scoundrel, I find that you hire your servants for *life*, and not by the month as I do; you are going straight to hell.

Paul. Never mind, Peter! That's my lookout. You hire your servants by the month or year, as may suit you best, and get away to heaven; but leave me to my own method.

Peter. No, I won't; I'll *beat your brains out!*

'And,' added Carlyle, 'has been trying dreadfully ever since, but has not yet been able to manage it,'—one of the most complete cases of begging the question and blinding the eyes with dust that I ever read. Did Carlyle forget, when he wrote that parable, that the negro had never been hired at all ; but that he had been *stolen*— basely stolen, nefariously stolen, sinfully stolen from his African home; and that for two hundred and fifty years the primal rights of manhood— the right to dispose of himself and his property as he saw fit—had been denied him? Did he forget, too, that to insult had been added *injury*, in beating, branding, cutting, wounding, lashing, lacerating, and a multitude of cruelties, such as break the spirits of those who are subject to them ? And did he forget once again that the *North did not begin the war*, but the South ; and that the North had been driven into it in sheer defence of the Union? How, there- fore, could he speak of Peter beating Paul's brains out, *because of a different system of hire ?*

But whilst slave-owners in America and slavery - sympathisers in England sought to embarrass the action of Lincoln by their time-

serving and mercenary counsels, there were not
wanting those, on both sides the Atlantic, who
cheered him on in the path of emancipation.
'Take me where I can see the battle,' said
a wounded soldier at the siege of Quebec; 'if
I cannot fight, I can cheer those who are
fighting.' 'Cheer him, cheer him!' said a man
in a crowd round a burning house, when he saw
one of the firemen trying to rescue a child, but
somewhat daunted by the flames; and a lofty
ringing cheer went up which so enheartened the
man that he made another attempt, and suc-
ceeded. And so Lincoln was enheartened in his
lofty but difficult emprise.

Among Americans who cheered him on we
find Henry Wadsworth Longfellow, Ralph
Waldo Emerson, Horace Greeley, James
Russell Lowell, Wendell Phillips; and last, but
not least, Harriet Beecher Stowe, whose work—
Uncle Tom's Cabin—'the most successful and
epoch-making romance ever written'—exercised
such a powerful influence on both sides of the
Atlantic. And among Englishmen we find
a vast body of working men — thousands of
whom, especially in Lancashire and Yorkshire,

suffered severely, almost excruciatingly, but bravely—headed by Richard Cobden and John Bright. These all took up the Bible refrain, and cried, 'Let My people go,' and again, 'Let My people go,' and again, like the replication of thunder in the mountains,

'LET MY PEOPLE GO!'

And Lincoln *did* let them go. By successive Acts of Congress, culminating in the Act of February 1st, 1865, and as a military expedient intended to crush a condition of armed rebellion, he

KNOCKED THE FETTERS FROM OFF FOUR MILLION SLAVES,

and sent them forth free men! Shortly after God smiled upon the Northern arms; the tide of battle turned; Richmond was evacuated; and the rebellion crushed.

Abraham Lincoln secured his object. He 'shot the rapids' of that stormy political period *without sinking the ship of State.* In order to do this, however, he had to *take God on board*— God Who had plans and purposes respecting a

subject race. Man proposed, but God disposed.
In and through all there was *a divine purpose*
running—lofty, humane, glorious!

> 'Sound the loud timbrel o'er Egypt's dark sea!
> Jehovah hath triumphed! His people are free!'

CONCLUSION.

'John Brown's body lies a-mouldering in the grave,
But his soul goes marching on.'

—Jubilee Melody.

'Lives of great men all remind us
    We can make our lives sublime,
And, departing, leave behind us
    Footprints on the sands of time.'

— Longfellow.

'The heroic example of other days is in great part the source
of the courage of each generation; and men walk up com-
posedly to the most perilous enterprises, beckoned onwards
by the shades of the brave that were.'

— Helps.

'Once to every man and nation comes the moment to
    decide,
In the strife of truth and falsehood, for the good and
    evil side;
Some great cause, God's new Messiah, offering each
    the bloom or blight,
Parts the goats upon the left hand, and the sheep
    upon the right,
And the choice goes by for ever 'twixt that darkness
    and that light.'

—Lowell.

    ' 'Tis ours to save our brethren, with peace and love to
        win
    Their darkened hearts from error, ere they harden
        them to sin.'

                                  —Lowell.

HONEST Abe and Brother Jim are dead. But the *cause* of *Humanity*—that cause for which they lived and laid down their lives — lives, and lives, I believe, in a loftier, grander, more hopeful condition because of their self-sacrificing toil. And now what I want is, that you young people should *take hold* of that cause. In its loftiest and best form, it is the cause of GOD. There is a story told of Abou Ben Adhem—how that one night, when praying, an angel appeared to him, writing in a book.

'What is it you write?' said Abou.

'The names of those who love God.'

'And is mine among them?'

'Nay.'

Whereupon Abou bowed his head and wept. Presently, recovering himself, he raised his head saying, ' If I be not among those who love God, please write me down as *one who loves his fellow-men.'* The angel did this and departed. Next night it reappeared,

> 'And show'd the names whom *love of God* had bless'd ;
> And lo ! Ben Adhem's name led all the rest.'

Yes! the cause of Humanity is the cause of God, and

> 'He's true to God who's true to man—wherever wrong is
> done,
> To the humblest and the weakest 'neath the all-beholding
> sun.'

Take up that cause, young men, and make it your own.

The task may be difficult. You may be *poor* and have your bread to win, or *obscure* and have your position to make. But the struggle for these, if rightly conducted, will fit you for higher struggles and nobler ends. Comparative poverty is wholesome. 'It is *twice* bless'd '—blessing him who is the subject of it, and those whom he may influence.

There is a story current of two children of two houses, each of whom wished to be at the top of a flight of stairs. The father of the first took the little thing in his strong arms, and without the slightest difficulty bore it thither. The other

father was wiser. He suffered his child to climb.
Slowly, patiently, step by step, did the boy toil
up the stairs. Every now and again he slipped
and had a little fall; but the father stood by, and
took care that he did not fall too far or hurt himself too much; and by and by he reached the
top. What was the result? The child who had
been carried to the top knew nothing of the
difficulty of getting there; he did not appreciate
his position, and he very speedily came neck-
break down; whereas the child who had toiled
there knew that every step had cost him a
struggle and a fear: he *did* appreciate his
position, and he *never lost it.*

That is a story, but it has been enacted in real
life many a time. Some fathers have toiled and
sweat, and almost died, to achieve position for
their children. The children, knowing little of
the difficulty, have not appreciated the position,
and have either lost it or been ruined by it. It's
a perilous thing for a boy to have the impression
that his father is very rich, that nothing depends
upon his own exertions, but that he may give
himself up to unlimited enjoyment. Work, hard
work—the sweat of the brain or the sweat of the

brow—may be a means of grace to you young
men.

And it may bless *others* through you.

The moral qualities of thoroughness, manliness, integrity, and righteousness—qualities which

LINCOLN CHOPPING WOOD.

stood the great Republic in such good stead at
the time of the rebellion — were tested and
strengthened in our heroes by the scenes and
associations of their manual toil. As a lad,
Lincoln did a great deal of tree - felling, rail-

splitting, and wood-cutting generally ; and with
reference to this it has been facetiously remarked,
that his knowledge of the different grains in the
wood enabled him to *polish the ebony case of the
negroes beautifully.* There is more than a play
upon words in that; there is a solid substratum
of truth. And *your* effort to win bread and
secure a position may be so conducted as to
develop character—character which may fit you
for higher service and extensive usefulness !

There are no slaves in England — of the
American type. There *are* slaves, though : men
who are tied and bound by the greed of their
fellows, and others who are in bondage to their
baser selves.

Slavery to the greed of others is seen in
connection with the *three great L's*—land, labour,
liquor. Man came from the land, lives on the
land, and in the end goes to the land. He
would therefore seem to have a natural and
indefeasible right in it. And yet in England—
a country of a population of over twenty million
souls—more than half the land is in the hands
of less than a thousand people ; and limitations
and restrictions are imposed upon its transfer—

not natural, but artificial—which make that transfer exceedingly difficult.

Labour, too, is necessary to enable us to appropriate the productions of the soil—to plough the field and scatter the good seed on the land, and to disinter the mineral wealth of the earth. Till recently, however, it received but scant recognition of its service. A better day has dawned; but further improvement would be an advantage. Perhaps we ought not seriously to interfere with the great natural law of demand and supply. But when *avarice* steps in and tries to wrest the law—takes advantage of the necessities of the poor to 'grind their faces,' and coin gold out of their very life - blood— there ought to be a public opinion sufficiently enlightened and strong to cry, Halt! If you cannot give a fair day's wages for a fair day's work, you are either incompetent or mean; in which case you are unfit to be an employer of labour in this last decade of the nineteenth Christian century.

The liquor question likewise needs looking to. Man has not only a right in the soil and a claim to its products, he has an interest in the

State and a claim on its protection. When the State, though, instead of prohibiting the traffic in folly and wickedness, practically encourages it—arms the men who engage in it with the authority of law — in lieu of protecting, it *persecutes* its children. The presence of so many licensed houses in our midst is a simple *infliction.* The State has no more right — natural or moral — to authorise public-houses and dancing-saloons, with their manifest encouragements to wine and lust, than it has to bring a desolating army over the land.

These monopolies and iniquities, which enrich the few at the expense and by the deep degradation of the many, must all be dealt with— effectually dealt with—ere it can be said

'There are no slaves in England;'

and when the time for dealing with them comes, you young men must be *ready,*—yea, you must *help to bring about the time !*

Don't be deterred by a false notion of *allegiance.*

'Are you pledged to craven silence? Oh, fling it to the wind,
The parchment wall that bars you from the least of human-kind—

That makes you cringe and temporise, and dumbly stand
    at rest,
While Pity's burning flood of words is red-hot in the
    breast !

Though you break your father's promise, you have nobler
    duties first ;
The traitor to Humanity is the traitor most accursed ;
Man is more than Constitutions ; better rot beneath the
    sod,
Than be true to Church and State while you are doubly
    false to God.

You owe allegiance to the State ; but deeper, truer, more
To the sympathies that God hath set within your spirit's
    core ;—
Your country claims your fealty ; I grant it so, but then
Before Man made you *citizens*, great Nature made you
    MEN.'

Still 'the soul of all improvement is the
improvement of the SOUL ; ' and, ere slavery
cease from beneath the British flag, men must
be freed as well from the baseness of themselves
as from the greed of their fellows. This baseness takes various forms—love of the wine-cup,
of the pleasures of sense, of the lusts of the flesh,
and of sinful indulgence generally. But whatever its form, it is characterised by one thing,
viz. *subordination of the lower to the higher*, the
better to the worse.

'It tumbles nature heel o'er head, and yelling with the
    yelling street,
Sets the feet above the brain, and swears the brain is in
    the feet.'

It is abnormal, unnatural, monstrous. FIGHT
IT !

That you may do this effectually, however,
you must first be free yourselves. The cry for
American freedom came not from the 'blacks'
but the ' whites.' The blacks—poor creatures!—
bowed by centuries of oppression, had ceased
to cry. They were enslaved mentally as well
as bodily ; and, left to themselves, they would
have been in bondage to-day. It was 'the
mean whites' as they were called by a mis-
judging selfishness—men who knew the joy
of liberty—who raised the cry, rent the air with
it, repeated and re-repeated it, and who, when
occasion was ripe, struck for and secured the
great boon. And if *you* would free your fellows
you must taste the sweets of liberty. This ' joy
of the Lord ' will be your '*strength*.' Come to
Jesus, then ! — to Him who is the TRUTH as
well as the Way and the Life, and whose
' Truth shall make you *free*.'

Then throw yourselves into the great struggle.

In the evening of the day on which the Ordinance of Secession was passed at South Carolina, 'a number of young men went to the churchyard, formed a circle round the grave of Mr. Calhoun—the great advocate of Southern privilege — and vowed to devote their lives, fortune, and honour to the independence of South Carolina'—really to the *continued enslavement of the 'blacks.'* Yours is nobler work —to *emancipate* and not enslave. With like determination, around the cross of Him who came 'to proclaim liberty to the captives, and the opening of the prison to them that are bound,' give yourselves to this work. The struggle may be arduous. The forces arrayed against you—drink, lust, gambling, greed, and that close-clinging carnality that 'is enmity against God' — are undoubtedly formidable. But they that be with you are more than they that be with them. Forward, then!

> 'Onward, while a wrong remains
>   To be conquered by the right—
> While oppression lifts a finger
>   To affront us by his might—
> While an error clouds the reason,
>   Or a sorrow gnaws the heart,
> Or a slave awaits his freedom—
>   *Action* is the wise man's part.'

Thus shall you help to bring about the time
—long prayed for and devoutly to be desired
—when not in England alone, but everywhere ;
not in a merely physical, but in a transcendently
higher sense, the sons of men shall stand up
in Christ redeemed, regenerated, and
DISENTHRALLED !

FINIS.

MORRISON AND GIBB, PRINTERS, EDINBURGH.

JOY OF HER HOME SERIES.

Small crown 8vo, Illustrated, cloth, gilt lettered, price 9d. each.

Honest Abe and Brother Jim: The two Martyred Presidents of the United States. By Rev. JOSHUA HAIGH.

Miss Dornwell's Domestic. By SARA MOORLAND.

Tom o' Jack's Lad. A Lancashire Story of the Days of John Wesley.

The Joy of Her Home. By L. J. TOMLINSON.

A-Fa: The Story of a Slave Girl in China.

Only a Ball. By JENNIE PERRETT.

Little Jim, a Young Christian Hero. By Rev. JOHN CLEGG.

Leaves from a Mission House in India.

Joe Webster's Mistake.

Sketches from My Schoolroom.

The Story of an Apprenticeship.

Broken. By EINAN.

Open Flowers, and Other Stories. By Mrs. HAYCRAFT.

Uncle Ray's Choice, and Other Stories. By JENNIE CHAPPELL.

Village Chimes, and Other Stories.

Short Sermons for Little People. By Rev. T. CHAMPNESS.

Mona Bell; or, Faithful over a Few Things.

Down and Up, and Other Stories. By OLIVER PACIS.

Clerk or Carpenter? A Story for Boys. By HARRIETT BOULTWOOD.

Next Door Neighbours. By R. F. HARDY.

Annals of Fairfield. By R. F. HARDY.

Two Little Wanderers. By R. F. HARDY.

Children of the Bible. Old Testament. By R. F. HARDY.

Pictures of Early Methodists for the Young. By ELLEN E. GREGORY.

Mary Ashton: A True Story of Eighty Years Ago.

Margaret Allerton. By A. M. WORKMAN.

The Boys of Northcote.

Dick's Troubles. By RUTH ELLIOTT.

John's Teachers. By LILLIE MONTFORT.

Ragged Jim's Last Song, and Other Ballads.

Nora Grayson's Dream.

Dots and Gwinnie.

Johnnie's Work, and How He did It.

Little Sally. By MINA E. GOULDING.

Minnie Neilson's Summer Holidays.

Pages from a Little Girl's Life.

Rosa's Christmas Invitations. By LILLIE MONTFORT.

The Wonderful Lamp, and Other Stories. By RUTH ELLIOTT.

The Wreck of the 'Maria' Mail Boat.

London: CHARLES H. KELLY, 2, Castle St., City Road, E.C.;
And 66, Paternoster Row, E.C.

www.ingramcontent.com/pod-product-compliance
Lightning Source LLC
Chambersburg PA
CBHW031442270326
41930CB00007B/828